From Swamp to Coal

From Swamp to Coal

Ali Mitgutsch

 Carolrhoda Books, Inc., Minneapolis

First published in the United States of America 1985 by Carolrhoda Books, Inc.
Original edition © 1984 by Sellier Verlag GmbH, Eching bei München,
West Germany, under the title VOM URWALD ZUR KOHLE.
Revised English text © 1985 by Carolrhoda Books, Inc.
Illustrations © 1984 by Sellier Verlag GmbH
All rights reserved.

Manufactured in the United States of America

LIBRARY OF CONGRESS CATALOGING IN PUBLICATION DATA

Mitgutsch, Ali.
   From swamp to coal.

     (A Carolrhoda start to finish book)
   Rev. English text of: Vom Urwald zur Kohle.
   SUMMARY: Describes how coal is formed by the earth and the methods used to mine it. Also discusses some of the uses of this mineral.

    1. Coal — Juvenile literature. [1. Coal]
I. Title.   II. Series.

TN799.5.M5813   1985   553.2′4   84-17465
ISBN 0-87614-233-1 (lib. bdg.)

1 2 3 4 5 6 7 8 9 10 94 93 92 91 90 89 88 87 86 85

From Swamp to Coal

The earth is very, very old.
For millions of years the land was covered
with swamps and forests.
Enormous trees grew in the forests.
Volcanoes spit out fire.
Earthquakes shook the earth.

The enormous trees got old and fell down.
New trees grew in their places.
Eventually they too got old and fell down.
In time the swamp bottoms filled up
with thick layers of rotten tree trunks.
With every earthquake
more and more earth was pushed over them.
The great weight of all this earth
pressed the layers of tree trunks tightly together.
The pressure was so great that the black rotten wood
became as hard as stone.
The wood had turned into coal.

Today coal lies beneath the ground in layers called **seams**, like the filling between layers in a chocolate cake.
Miners dig underground to get out the coal.
First a shaft is dug down to a seam.
Then a tunnel is dug sideways into the seam.
Mines grow deeper and longer as miners dig out more coal.

In the old days, miners dug with picks and shovels.
Often they had to work lying down
because the tunnels were so low.
Today machines dig most of the coal from the tunnel walls.

The loose coal is loaded into **shuttle cars** which are rolled into an elevator called a **cage**. Then the cage is hauled up the shaft to the surface.

Above ground the coal cars are emptied into a big funnel.
Then the coal is poured into railroad cars
so it can be shipped to coal yards or power plants.

Today most coal is burned in power plants.
The coal fire boils water to make steam.
The steam drives big engines, called **turbines**,
that generate electricity.
This electricity flows through power lines
to factories, businesses, and houses.

In our homes electricity runs vacuum cleaners
and refrigerators and washing machines.
It lights up our rooms at the flick of a switch.
It brings life into our TV sets and radios.
In addition to providing us with electrical power,
coal is used to make perfumes, tennis rackets, plastic seats,
caps for toothpaste tubes, and much, much more.
Our lives wouldn't be the same without it.

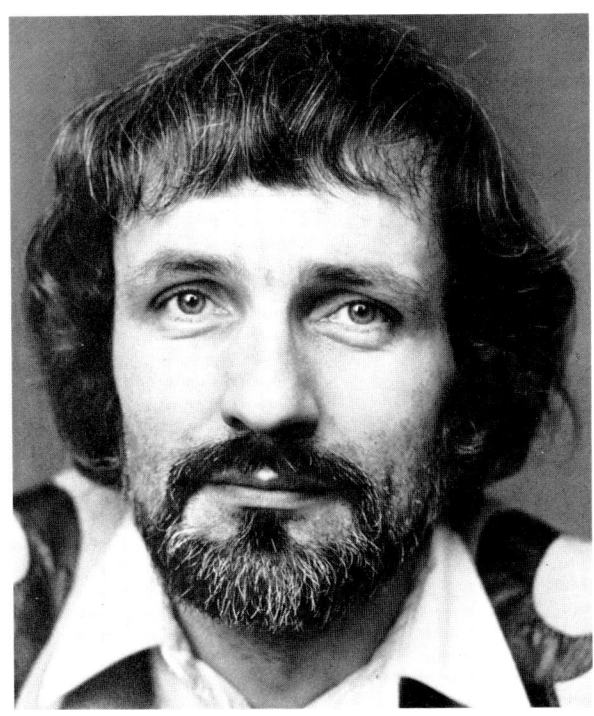

Ali Mitgutsch

ALI MITGUTSCH is one of Germany's best-known children's book illustrators. He is a devoted world traveler, and many of his book ideas have taken shape during his travels. Perhaps this is why they have such international appeal. Mr. Mitgutsch's books have been published in 22 countries and are enjoyed by thousands of readers around the world.

Ali Mitgutsch lives with his wife and three children in Schwabing, the artists' quarter in Munich. The Mitgutsch family also enjoys spending time on their farm in the Bavarian countryside.

THE CAROLRHODA
 **START**

From Beet to Sugar	NEW From Graphite to Pencil
From Blossom to Honey	From Grass to Butter
From Cacao Bean to Chocolate	From Ice to Rain
From Cement to Bridge	From Milk to Ice Cream
From Clay to Bricks	From Oil to Gasoline
From Cotton to Pants	From Ore to Spoon
From Cow to Shoe	From Sand to Glass
From Dinosaurs to Fossils	NEW From Sea to Salt
From Egg to Bird	From Seed to Pear
From Egg to Butterfly	From Sheep to Scarf
From Fruit to Jam	NEW From Swamp to Coal
NEW From Gold to Money	From Tree to Table
From Grain to Bread	

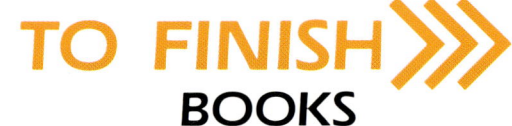
TO FINISH BOOKS